ale(theia)

Kripi Malviya

Hawakal Publishers

Published by Hawakal Publishers, 185 Kali Temple Road,
Nimta, Kolkata 700049

Email: info@hawakal.com

Website: www.hawakal.com

First edition (India): March, 2018
Copyright © Kripi Malviya 2018
Cover art: Srijoni Manna
Cover designed by Chitrangi
Author photograph: Natalie Lycops

ISBN: 978-93-87883-02-4 (Paperback)

Price: INR 150.00 | USD 6.50

Dedicated to *Kavita*—the *Maa*, the poet and the poem

PREFACE

In the summer of 2017 *Rhythm Divine Poets* (RDP) initiated perhaps India's first ever poetry chapbook contest. This ambitious project to recognize and publish new and upcoming poets saw participation by poets from all over the world. It was followed by the arduous task of judging the manuscripts by three noted poets: Sanjukta Dasgupta, Sharmila Ray and Kushal Poddar. After almost a year-long process of longlisting and shortlisting the final results were declared in January 2018 where Huzaifa Pandit and Kripi Malviya came out winners. A cover art contest too was conducted which was judged by eminent painters Partha Roy and Sudhangsu Bandyopadhyay where the art works of Srijoni Manna, Pradnya Kushal and Niloy Kanti Biswas were declared the winners. Two of those three artworks form the cover images of the two chapbooks. Rhythm Divine Poets are fortunate to have the services of *Hawakal Publishers* who agreed to publish the two winners of this contest.

According to Sanjukta Dasgupta discovering new poetic talent has been a matter of great excitement and joy because the contest has amply proved that poetry in English in the 21st century is journeying into unprecedented terrains. Sharmila Ray acknowledges that poetry cannot be judged but she was again amazed at the transformative powers of words hence language. Reading the poems she was teased, troubled, enlightened and joyous. She believes that poetry is a metaphor not only to express the reality we are in but it also helps to build how we

5

perceive reality and in these trying times we need it more than ever. Kushal Poddar realized that poetry contest results are the result of a momentary avowal or denial, a bend in the river. Judging the chapbook contest was an opportunity to step outside his comfort zone as a reader.

Rhythm Divine Poets, co-founded by three Kolkata-based poets Amit Shankar Saha, Sufia Khatoon and Anindita Bose, has over the period of three years since its inception, worked for the promotion of poetry through various activities like events, workshops, publications, and giving platforms to young and aspiring poets. Currently the group has three youth coordinators, Nikita Parik, Ruth Pal Chaudhuri and Sanjukta Sarkar, who work tirelessly to bring the vision of the group into a reality. The group has utilized the advantages of social networks like WhatsApp, Facebook and Blogs (http://rhythmdivinepoets.blogspot.in) to create the so-called "poetry scene" and the success of this poetry chapbook contest is evidence of that effort.

The group thanks the judges, *Hawakal Publishers*, and all those who came in support of the endeavour. *Rhythm Divine Poets* wishes the two winning poets the very best in their poetic journey in life.

RDP
March 23, 2018
Calcutta, India

"aletheia" is an ancient Greek word meaning unconcealed, unclosedness, disclosure or truth; reflections of the striving created through the poet's allegiance to existential philosophy and psychotherapy. "theia" is a hypothesized ancient planetary-mass object in the early solar system, and it is believed that the moon was formed by a violent, head-on collision between the early Earth and a "planetary embryo" (theia) approximately one hundred million years after the Earth formed. The title of the chapbook wanted to portray the author's preoccupations and yearnings that are rooted in beliefs and searches of wildly unique worlds, both within and without, ultimately shedding light on her poetry writing process. "ale(theia)" is a dedication to the intimate unraveling of the geography, anatomy and vulnerability of the encounters in the author's life.

ACKNOWLEDGEMENTS

The poem "To the Fore" was first published in *The Psychedelic Press*, UK. The poems "Noon Wind," and "Deadlock" were first published in *The Four Quarters Magazine*. The poems "Structures," "Palate," "Isochronic," "The S Bend," "Vertigo," and "Sans Titre" were first published in *The Sunflower Collective*.

I thank Kiriti Sengupta for agreeing to write the blurb for my book. I thank *Rhythm Divine Poets* and *Hawakal Publishers* for publishing my first collection of poems.

CONTENTS

Part 1: Thailand

Sans Titre   11
Deadlock   12
To The Fore   13
Structures   14
Palate   15
Noon Wind   16
The S Bend   17
Isochronic   18
Vertigo   19

Part 2: Finland

Corrade   21
Primeval   22
Pan   23
Mielikki   24
Taiga   25
Asterism   26
Phobos And Deimos   27
Ilmarinen   28
Somesthesia   29
Seism   30
Solitons   31
Thenar   32
Synty   33
Tounela   34
Narskunta   35

PART 1: THAILAND

SANS TITRE

he is weathered man, hands burnt with powdered
snow
she is learning to separate her bones from the bed
sheets that hold blue panic

he is anger resembling the after currents of a seabed
earthquake
she is red surging rage as if to cover the empty graves
of the earth

he shoots feathered arrows for truths
she explodes for each silenced life

he answers five am cries of pain
she appears at the ankles of the fallen

he is water-colour of natural disasters
she is oil strokes of dis-proportionate scales

he is a taster of chemically induced despair caves
she is spontaneous rock formations found in the
violent aftermath of life-death cycles

he is the resolution
she is the skin rising

he is the false evidence of justified crime
she is living of the impoverished edges of bloodlines

DEADLOCK

Cleave the tornado
Leave no other, no self
Mould, no earth core
Shared walls are fearsome
of the morphine voices
No separateness found in the buried ice
Metals, manipulated
Set into millions of cube homes but
The sky still reigns in its neverness
They swallow one another as
The telephone screams
Hot tears return, blind and violet
Vanilla vanity and
Soul architects of skin covered pulsars
We know no white beginnings

TO THE FORE

giddy as fractals from
my kaleidoscopic eyes
I wait, pretend, prolong, push

for not a place
and definitely not for the human
and not just for desolation, despair or ecstasy

but for an empty stomach
half broken glass of white noise,
an intricate study of how pebbles are stones,
split ends, the smell of your day old breath,
concentrated *dhyaan* of broken skin

for making sense of fear
but not making any sense at all
for lucid lies of art,
and forgotten senses emerging
that mock all realisations

for the luxury of written hurt
For spontaneous sleep;
elusive like a drunken dream

for the convulsing sobs of time passing
for every now that has ever been

STRUCTURES

Kingfisher wing child,
Radiant maa is in
all my summers

Yearning water youth,
the colossal empathy
of hair rising for rover winter

Life created at the continent's edge
Power lines running on skin

Both sides of my teeth
are acquainted with you

Keep the mountain in your mouth
Stop the anarchy of the forgotten

PALATE

I, radical machinery
Conifer and concrete anatomy
Skylark motorcycle heat rising

I, triumph of barefoot wet streets
Mourning long hair and
Distant railway lines
Arched muscles
rapt quivering teeth

I, rear viewer
queer queen
Silent speed musician
Bone spear scream

NOON WIND

sick steps going to a plateau
threatening tides of a different storm
we will be blown in search
of another uninhabitable planet
until the earthquake called fear
swirls inside this mountain

THE S BEND

Staring at stranger
dissolution

Of lines, hair
grinding teeth

Birds of prey
years of days

The united colours
of naked

In the darkening,
touch rejection

Homes are
moving

Simultaneous ornate
recall associations

Fishnet skin
clouds lay bare

ISOCHRONIC

Saturate awe
Endlessly touch the silent
Remember your groans

Keep the damp
You lone life berg
Sharply inhale dispersion

Trace your burns
Let them know your glow
Your flaking skinned fingers

The familiar light song
Imploding into mother
Learn the choke of home

VERTIGO

This street is a force
holding our spines in its derision
between muscles soaked in black oil

The unexpected loss of light from the eyes
is known to all rivers as they declare
their borrowed stillness in our cupped hands

In the endless landscape of the senses
we learn the true unarming of our time

PART 2: FINLAND

CORRADE

I wish we always loved
the way we love
when we leave

there is a sound that lips make
when they receive
and sever;

some call it rainfall
I think it's lapsing in the straits of loss,
argent grass blades yielding

PRIMEVAL

raid in the internal rain
on this failed star
that is our boundary

PAN

the first light of restraint
white peaks, white hair

waking as rasping in slipstream;
blue light wind

granite tears held at canthus,
at the apex of our anatomies

we are not coated in land
but in spillage and storm

reliving lunate;
I can be found in the rapids of the day

in the caesura of moisture,
and the reflections of ira

MIELIKKI

She holds herself often
Small veins under translucent skin hide on the sides
of her forehead
until the sky hair allow them to be seen

It's difficult to tell whether the purple on her eyelids
are her own
or something she takes on from the lakes
but they cause a hailstorm when you look at her just
the same

It's hard to look at her.
Like taking in all of her at the same time
will root your muscles to her ashen ground

I have seen the flow of her rivers now
and there are few things so clear and brilliant
as her motion

She is watchful, the forest maiden,
watchful of her hidden terrors
and of yours, if you look hard enough

She holds herself often
and she folds you too,
taking whole northlands with her

TAIGA

Consider excavation of our biomes
Dyspneal as religion
Motionless as prayer

If I could, I would
enclose you as a clearing in a pine night before true
spring

Holding as flexure, as embedded skin
at the nervure of the flightless

ASTERISM

we osculate,
puller and stealth
bare trees on empurpled days that end too late

lake layers on fovea
unattainable, valved—
our theatre of war

ramous urges
she sweats and rises still
in his terraqueous grit

PHOBOS AND DEIMOS

on their cratered kind
rover hunters quarry
wake-less dissenters

ILMARINEN

bending weight as a habit
sizing the sky that falls,
that falls to your folded knees

unmake the bed
and spread it out again
for our motion, our limbs soldered
inflammable, conjoint

let's walk
the distance where we are invisible
where we are audible with volition
while my drink gets warmer
waiting for me to melt away from you

our bare skin ascending to no skin
and you noticing it all even in your spent after,
as in our empty—we forge

SOMESTHESIA

Stratus descendants;
we learned to walk
on wingspan quasars

SEISM

bitter trails on naked grail
you tilt to drench in them
and break yourself
on her laminae

bending under star burns
she wants her blood shells to hesitate
so she can hear your satellites
and hold a mouthful of post extinguished stares

the shuttle lost power
at the inclines of her hair
sharp canines for your marauding tongue
roaring the instinct to cascade

talking only to be closer
to the shadow of her feet
what makes her tremble?

SOLITONS

they unfold in sarsar
these fictile goddesses
and suspend you on their crest

THENAR

with intent, i unearth
your fervid flood
your trench warfare
your pulseless

with pulsar pace,
reave your night vision
eat into your reticence
fill your moon quakes

and only then,
return you back to yourself
heaving, cored, afire
a sweltering vale

SYNTY

Half levitate and slam back into
this encrusted curved heath of a body
this voltaic enclosure of our collisions
this undertide of deities

TOUNELA

Scrape this skin,
the veiled cambers

Pause the kiln
Swirl and forget to exhale

There is no outside,
only labial gasps

Aligned utterances on the floor

NARSKUNTA

Blood obscure between the eyes of trees
White invasions of sound, of incantations
I will meet you on the volcano of mute